A CELEBRATION OF PRAISE

An original collection of poems, giving praise and glory to God!!

Vicklyn Thomas

Praise the Lord.

Praise the Lord, you His servants;
praise the name of the Lord.

Let the name of the Lord be praised,
both now and forever more.

From the rising of the sun to the place where it sets,
the name of the Lord is to be praised.

The Lord is exalted over all the nations,
His glory above the heavens.

Who is like our God, the One who sits enthroned on high,
Who stoops down to look on the heavens and the earth?

He raises the poor from the dust and lifts the needy
from the ash heap; He seats them with princes,
with the princes of His people.

He settles the childless woman in her home
as a happy mother of children.

Praise the Lord.
(Psalm 113:1-9 Today's New International Version)

A Celebration of Praise

United States Copyright Office - 1-366-650
Copyright © 2007

All rights reserved. No part of this book may be reproduced, stored in a retrieval system or transmitted in any form or by any means, electronic, mechanical, photocopying, recording or otherwise, without the written permission of the copyright owner.

Layout and design by Vicklyn Thomas
www.vickiesvizions.com

Printed in the United States of America
By Lulu
www.lulu.com

ISBN 978-0-6151-8522-4

Dedication

This book is dedicated to
some very special people

To my husband **David**:
He has been my most avid supporter
for as long as I have known him.
He has encouraged me with all the fervor
and passion that he possesses.
When I doubted I could do it, he was
there right beside me, speaking God's
word over me and urging me on.

To my children: **Rachel and Chad:**
They always say, "Mummy you can do it."

I celebrate my family and praise God
for giving them to me.

Vickie

A CELEBRATION OF PRAISE
≅ Table of Contents ≅
Dedication

The Sweetest Praise	1
Patiently Waiting	2
God's Word	3
God's Love	4
The Hand of God	5
The Whisper of His Grace	6
Isn't It Amazing?	7
That First Easter	8
I Wasn't There	9
Fruits of the Spirit	10
Happiness	11
Let Me Bloom Where I Am Planted	12
Lord, Thank You	13
He That Hath Ears	14
Don't Turn Your Back on God	15
I Never Want to Live Without You, Lord	16
The Steps of a Godly Woman	17
My Prayer List	18
My Heavenly Outfit	19
Celebration of Praise	20

From My Heart

From a very young age, poetry attracted me. If anything happened at all, especially during my high-school years, I expressed it in poetry. If it was a funny incident at school or home, I would write a poem about it and long after it happened, that poem would become a reminder.

Since writing was one of my hobbies, it was easy for me to write poetry. As long as the words were coming, I would write. I remember the last poem that I wrote and read was at my high school graduation .

Somehow over the years, even though I still read a lot of poetry, I stopped writing. I am not sure what caused that, but I did. However, I always felt that it was just there waiting to get out.

Eventually, a few years ago, the Holy Spirit started to impress on my heart to write a few poems for my family and give them as gifts. That gave me such a release. It was so satisfying to see what I felt in writing. Since then, I have penned many more poems, and plan to continue writing as long as God places the words on my heart.

*This first book of poetry is a **Celebration of Praise** to God for all that He has done so far in my life and all that He promises to do.*

Thank you friends and family, for your support on this journey. May this work truly bless your hearts and inspire you to celebrate who Jesus is and all He has done for you.

1.
<u>THE SWEETEST PRAISE</u>

How sweet the atmosphere that praise
Creates and also forms,
It's such a rich enduring place,
That strays away from the norm.

Our praise is like a sweet perfume,
Like flowers when they bloom,
And when we open up that door,
Christ gladly enters the room.

His word says that He loves our praise,
He accepts all we give,
For praise is saying, Welcome Lord,
I want You here to live.

God loves our praise, He's made it clear,
That it's a great delight,
To hear His children bless His name,
Every day and every night.

Our praise can bring God on the scene,
Our thanks can move His hand,
Praise dispels fears, erases doubts,
In ways we can't understand.

When darkness like a heavy cloak
Surrounds us day and night,
The penetrating force of praise,
Brings forth a welcome light.

Praise as a weapon can be used,
To fight the enemy's attack,
Its strength can upset any plan,
And push the forces back.

The praise and worship that we send,
Just magnifies His name,
It gives us strength and energy,
Our lives are not the same.

Oh Jesus! is our sweetest praise,
Oh God! our earnest cry,
Let's not forget to reverence Him,
And lift His name up high.

♦

2.
PATIENTLY WAITING

Waiting calls for patience,
I know that is the key,
So I may receive everything,
That my God has for me.

New or old my petitions,
Whatever the time frame,
I believe my breakthrough only comes,
By meditating on His names.

He is **Jehovah-Nissi**,
The Lord my cover, my banner,
Love, comfort and also shelter,
He provides in an awesome manner.

He is **Jehovah-Rapha**,
The Lord that healeth me,
So if I'm sick in body or mind,
That disease has got to flee.

He is **Jehovah-Jireh**,
The one who provides for me,
No matter what needs I possess,
My source He'll always be.

He is **Jehovah-Shammah**,
The Lord is always there,
There's no place I can hide from Him,
His presence ever near.

He is **Jehovah-Shalom**,
Forever He will be my peace,
In the midst of trial, in the midst of storm,
At His voice the raging must cease.

⇔

Emmanuel; God is with us,
A close and faithful friend,
Who promises never to leave or forsake,
He'll be with me to the end.

Our God is a Deliverer,
A mighty Fortress is He,
A shield and buckler, Ancient of Days,
A God of Sovereignty.

The God of the Old Testament,
Abraham, Moses and Isaac,
Has proven He's my shepherd,
As His child I never lack.

Any time that we grow weary,
While waiting on the Lord,
His character surely always proves,
He's a God who keeps His word.

There's strength for all who are waiting,
Like eagles they will soar,
No tiredness, no weary arms,
No cop-out, no detour.

Rest on His promises while waiting,
Meditating o'er and o'er,
Knowing that the Lord of Lords, the King of Kings,
Will come through like He has before.

When I think of God's true character,
And I look at my different needs,
There's an overwhelming assurance,
That HE is the answer indeed.

3.
*G*OD'S *W*ORD

God's word, it feeds the hungry soul,
And soothes the aching heart,
It's hope for who have lost their way,
And gives a brand new start.

It's life for those who just exist,
A delight to meditate,
You're sure to find all that you need,
To satisfy any state.

It's a compass for the traveler,
For the homeless it's a home,
It's comfort for the wounded mind,
A rest for those who roam.

Its wisdom is immeasurable,
Its instruction has no end,
With it there's no comparison,
Not one part needs amend.

Like exercise for the physical,
It gives life to your spirit,
Bend it, stretch it, test its strength,
To feel renewed and energetic.

Raised as a standard against the enemy,
It shields and it protects,
Just speak it with authority,
And see some amazing effects.

It's hard sometimes to understand,
The choices we should make,
But if we look to this powerful word,
We'll know the path to take.

Make it a part of your daily life,
Breathe it like clean fresh air,
Keep it hidden in your heart,
And take it everywhere.

♦

4.
GOD'S LOVE

God's love, I can't, I won't compare
To that of any other,
It's high above and far exceeds,
That of sister, mother or brother.

It makes me feel so wanted,
So cherished, I'm so loved,
I'm filled with awesome wonder,
At that great love from above.

It's hard to even fathom,
How He could take my place
And give the life, the life He owned,
That I could see His face.

There's none that I could think of,
Would give their all for me,
Oh God, please keep me in that love,
Through all eternity.

◆

5.
THE HAND OF GOD

I'm awed at God's creation,
Amazed by His designs,
My thoughts are filled with wonder,
I'm so enthralled it boggles my mind.

I see the stars in their glory,
The moon in visible splendor,
The sun that overshadows us,
The earth with all its grandeur.

I think the Hand that holds them,
For all the world to see,
Must surely be a marvel,
To display such perfect beauty.

Then my thoughts go back to Calvary,
The day those hands were outstretched,
As they bore the pain and sorrow,
For me who is such a wretch.

I fall to my knees before Him,
And with feebleness I pray,
Thank you Lord for that moment,
When you washed my sins away.

Your hands that have such power,
To form the earth and sky,
Could reach down when I was lonely,
And lovingly draw me nigh.

I'm still amazed at Your Greatness,
To hold the world in Your Hand,
My heart with joy, will surely sing,
When before Your face I stand.

♦

6.
THE WHISPER OF HIS GRACE

I hear the whistling of the breeze,
And feel its gentle touch,
The tiny rustling of the leaves,
It moves them, oh so much.

I am reminded of God's grace,
As gentle as that breeze,
It cradles me with loving arms,
And puts my soul at ease.

I feel His hand still leading,
As I go along life's race,
My soul is always listening for,
The whisper of His grace.

When I think I cannot make it,
And I may not see His face,
His word always remind me of,
The whisper of His grace.

He says it is sufficient,
To keep me in this place,
I never need to hunger for,
The whisper of His grace.

No way that I could earn it,
Whether fast or slow my pace,
And so I'm truly thankful for,
The whisper of His grace.

◆

7.
Isn't It Amazing?

Isn't it amazing,
The earth, the sky, the sea?
Isn't it amazing,
The flower, the bird, the bee?

Isn't it amazing,
The hand, the eye, the mind?
Isn't it amazing,
About God, about mankind?

Isn't it amazing,
To see, to hear, to talk?
Isn't it amazing,
To jump, to skip, to walk?

Isn't it amazing,
To read, to learn, to know?
Isn't it amazing,
To eat, to sleep, to grow?

Isn't it amazing,
The rain, the sleet, the snow?
Isn't it amazing,
A hurricane, an earthquake, a tornado?

Isn't it amazing,
That God created all these glories?
Isn't it amazing,
They're real, and not mere stories?

Isn't it amazing,
Even before the world was formed?
Isn't it amazing,
God knew when and where we'd be born?

Isn't it amazing,
God the Father, Son and Spirit?
Isn't it amazing,
God's word and the power within it?

Isn't it amazing,
That for all the world to see?
Isn't it amazing,
How Christ went to Calvary?

Isn't it amazing,
That He laid down His life?
Isn't it amazing,
There would be such a sacrifice?

I find it so amazing,
Still I know God's word is true.
He said if I confess, He'd dwell with me,
I've done it, how about you?

♦

8.
THAT FIRST EASTER

He stood alone that first Easter,
Hanging from the cross,
When He gave His very life's blood,
To save and redeem the lost.

His Father couldn't stand it,
To see Him on the tree,
And caused Him to cry in anguish,
Why has Thou forsaken me?

The soldiers, they were laughing,
As they mocked and spat on Him,
So ignorant were their actions,
They didn't know it was their sin.

Their sin and everyone else's,
Had caused Him so much pain,
We caused our Lord and Savior,
To bear unspeakable shame.

That day the enemy was smiling,
When He saw Christ's blood was shed,
But there was rejoicing in heaven,
When Christ crushed the serpent's head.

It was love that drove Him to Calvary,
That caused God to take such action,
But with joy we want to declare,
Hallelujah! There was resurrection.

◆

9.
I Wasn't There

I wasn't there that first Easter,
When He prayed, God's only son,
When He said to His loving Father,
Thy will, not mine be done.

I wasn't there when the soldiers
Came and arrested my Lord,
When they falsely accused my Savior,
Of preaching a heathen word.

I wasn't there when they nailed Him,
To a cross He had to bear,
When they spat and mocked in anger,
And it seemed like no one cared.

I wasn't there when that cross got heavy,
The heaviest ever it seemed,
When by the plan of the Master,
Along came Simon of Cyrene.

But by faith I saw when they cast lots,
As the word had said they would,
And they laughed at Christ our Savior,
As He gave His precious blood.

By faith I saw when they pierced Him,
And the blood came from His side,
And He looked in love, not anger,
On those for whom He died.

I wasn't there to see the lightning,
Or the temple's veil rent in twain,
But by faith I heard the thunder,
As each clap echoed His pain.

By faith my heart that was broken,
Was glued together and healed,
That day He went to Calvary,
My future and fate was sealed.

No one who says they love us,
Would ever do such a thing,
Open your heart to the Savior,
Who just longs to come in.

By faith He asks us to trust Him,
To let Him keep us from strife,
Take His hand, walk beside Him,
And experience abundant life.

♦

10.

F<small>RUITS</small> OF THE S<small>PIRIT</small>

Let love, let hope, let peace and joy,
Be evermore your friends,
Let goodness, mercy, hope and grace,
Stay with you to the end.

Let love replace a hardened heart,
And peace a troubled mind,
Let tenderness, patience, guide your hands,
But don't leave joy behind.

For if you keep these spiritual truths,
A part of your life always,
Success will be yours, favor for sure,
Until the end of your days.

◆

11.

<u>HAPPINESS</u>

Happiness is a state of mind,
Not based on happenings,
It's a deep-seated joy,
That's found in God,
No matter if you lose or win.

Happiness is a contented state,
Reflected from deep inside,
It's a faith in God,
Reserved for those,
Who in His love abide.

◆

12.
LET ME BLOOM WHERE I AM PLANTED

Let me bloom where I am planted,
Lord, let me lift my voice,
When everyone chooses to follow,
Help me to make a choice.

Let me bloom where I am planted,
Let me stand for what is right,
When those around grow weary,
Let my lamp be oh so bright.

Let me bloom where I am planted,
An example of Your grace,
When everything seems dismal,
There's still a smile upon my face.

Let me bloom where I am planted,
With a humble heart, not proud,
Let me come away, be separated,
And stand out from the crowd.

Let me bloom where I am planted,
In a world that's dying in sin,
Let my life show that You're able,
To change us from within.

Let me bloom where I am planted,
As I spread Your love around,
I'll be a sweet, sweet smell in Your nostrils,
That rises up from the ground.

Let me bloom where I am planted,
And lift Your name in praise,
Your greatness I'll shout forever,
Over and over my voice I will raise.

♦

13.
LORD, THANK YOU

Lord, thank You for my trials,
My tears, Lord, and my pain,
For they're the only reasons,
That so much I have gained.

Lord, thank you for every heartache,
And for each crushing blow,
That forced me to look deep inside,
And help me, Lord, to grow.

Lord, thank you for every midnight,
When darkness stretched so long,
Then the precious name of Jesus,
Became my one and only song.

Lord, thank you for each promise,
You gave me through it all,
Your love became my cushion
And a soft place I could fall.

Lord, thank You.

♦

14.
HE THAT HATH EARS

That's not for me, was your reply,
When God first called on you,
I'm qualified for something else,
I'll choose what I want to do.

Again God said, come here my child,
There's work over here to be done,
You said, wait Lord, I'll be right back,
I have to look after my son.

Still God gave you another chance,
To help affect some change,
O Lord, assign me somewhere else,
These people are really strange.

So God decided enough is enough,
I'm going out to the street,
To bring in the poor, the lame, the blind,
And the one who has nothing to eat.

I'll call on those that you despise,
And those that you overlook,
Tell them come, for my house shall be filled,
Every corner, every cranny, every nook.

If any man chooses to come to me,
And hate not the life he had before,
He cannot sit at my table,
No he can't come in that door.

For whosoever does not bear his cross,
To walk and follow after Me,
Isn't fit for the kingdom of God,
My disciple he can never be.

When God chooses to call on you,
Maybe soon, maybe some time next year,
Before you say no, remember His word,
He that hath ears, let him hear.

◆

15.
DON'T TURN YOUR BACK ON GOD

Peter said, "There's no way, Lord,
I'll turn my back on you,"
But Jesus said, "Before sunrise,
That's exactly what you will do."

And sure enough as Jesus said,
Before the rooster crowed thrice,
Peter had denied the Lord,
When fear gripped him like a vice.

How many times, just like Peter,
We've promised Christ the same,
Then one look from the enemy,
Makes us deny His name.

We proclaim we would serve the Lord,
Since He's done so much for us,
But then when life is smooth again,
From Him we remove our trust.

If we deny Him on this earth,
He said He'll do the same,
Before His Father up in heaven,
He won't remember our names.

How good it would be if the Lord,
Each time He had something to say,
Knew that He could depend on us,
To listen and then to obey.

God has been faithful every time
We've turned our hearts to Him,
We can't let trials weaken us,
Nor make our faith grow dim.

He promised He wouldn't give us more,
Than we could ever bear,
All He asked is for us to lay down,
Our burdens and our cares.

Open your mouth and boldly proclaim
Of the God in whom you delight,
Don't grow weary, don't compromise,
Don't ever hide your light.

Come, stand your ground, declare your faith,
In whom you have believed,
Let nothing, no one, distract you,
And your blessing you will receive.

♦

16.
I Never Want To Live Without You, Lord

I never want to live without You, Lord,
I need you every day,
I never want to live without You, Lord,
For me, You are the way.

I never want to live without You, Lord,
The thought fills me with fear,
I never want to live without You, Lord,
Your love, I want to share.

I never want to live without You, Lord,
Your love just fills my heart,
I never want to live without You, Lord,
You keep me from falling apart.

I never want to live without You, Lord,
For my life I'd make a mess,
I never want to live without You, Lord,
You're my answer for the stress.

I never want to live without You, Lord,
Your Word, it is my hope,
I never want to live without You, Lord,
Your strength helps me to cope.

I never want to live without You, Lord,
I'll always hold Your hand,
I never want to live without You, Lord,
I will follow Your command.

I never want to live without You, Lord,
You mean the world to me,
I never want to live without You, Lord,
Forever, this is my decree.

◆

The following poem and bookmark were written to correspond with the theme for a women's weekend retreat.

"The Steps of a Godly Woman."

The poem is partially based on **Proverbs 31,** with the encouragement that every woman who submits to the power of the Holy Ghost can walk in absolute victory.

I want to encourage anyone who reads this, woman or man, old or young, to personalize it and see yourself walking **in sync with God's heartbeat.**

Walking by faith,
not by sight.

Obedient to
His every call,

Moving in steps,
He has ordered.

Acknowledging that,
He knows it all.

New heights, new
depths, new strength.

17.
THE STEPS OF A GODLY WOMAN

The steps of a Godly woman,
Are surely ordered by God,
His word lights up her pathway,
No matter where she trod.

In all her ways she acknowledges,
His knowledge and His strength,
To do His will, to seek His face,
She will go to any length.

A strong woman is greatly admired,
But a Godly woman much more,
For she carries inside her God's presence,
Her walk says, "It's Him I adore."

She wears God's wisdom like rubies,
His understanding covers her like gold,
She's dressed for success,
on His principles she rests,
As she takes His hand in a firm hold.

Her words extol His praises,
For it's her pure delight,
To see her with both hands outstretched,
Is such a glorious sight.

She yields her will at His prodding,
Holds on even through the pain,
In her closet she kneels,
and it's there He reveals,
If you lose all for Me you will gain.

She's an inspiration to those around her,
For she has learnt the fear of the Lord,
By holding His hand, obeying His command,
Her life often free from discord.

The steps of a Godly woman,
Are in-sync with God's heartbeat,
His wish, her desire, as she humbly aspires,
To forever kneel at His feet.

◆

Lord, our Lord, how majestic is Your name in all the earth!

You have set Your glory above the heavens.

Through the praise of children and infants, You have established a stronghold against Your enemies, to silence the foe and the avenger.

When I consider Your heavens, the work of Your fingers, the moon and the stars, which You have set in place,

What are mere mortals that You are mindful of them, human beings that You care for them?

You have made them a little lower than the heavenly beings and crowned them with glory and honor.

You made them rulers over the works of Your hands; You put everything under their feet:

All flocks and herds, and the animals of the wild, the birds in the sky, and the fish in the sea, all that swim the paths of the seas.

Lord, our Lord, how majestic is Your name in all the earth!

Psalm 8....Today's New International Version

The next two poems were birthed during my personal devotion time one morning. The first one, "My Prayer List," came to me while I sat contemplating what and whom I should pray about that morning. I really wanted my time with God to be full and productive. Realizing that I had a lot to pray about, I thought I should write it all down so I wouldn't forget and in doing so, the idea for this poem came.

After spending time in prayer, I read a portion from Ephesians 6, and while meditating on it, the second poem, "My Heavenly Outfit," started taking shape. After reading it many times over, I realize how important it is to wear my heavenly armor all the time.

18.
<u>My Prayer List</u>

I stood and thought for a moment,
The things I needed to pray about,
I felt I should get a notebook,
And write each and every one out.

For it came to me in an instant,
And I felt that the list would be long,
So I knew I had such a huge task,
To make things right that were wrong.

I started first with my family,
The ones who were close to me,
I jotted their names on my notepad,
That made up my first list of three.

I prayed for their protection,
I prayed to God for their strength,
And because I really love them,
Those prayers had quite some length.

I spent some time on my husband,
Declaring God's word over him,
I prayed he'd serve God so faithful,
Even when his eyes have grown dim.

I then switched to my children,
And I lifted them up too,
To God an earnest petition,
That their love would always be new.

I prayed about my nephew and sister,
They'd soon open their hearts,
To Jesus as Lord and Master,
He would give them a brand new start.

My next focus was my brother,
I knew He always acknowledged the Lord,
I believed some day not too far off,
He'd be out proclaiming the Word.

I didn't forget my mother,
If I did my list wouldn't be complete,
O God, I said, please save her,
Keep her strong and keep her sweet.

My thoughts traveled to my relatives,
Those far and those who lived near,
I placed this request before Him,
Please keep them each day of the year.

I couldn't forget my husband's family,
For he had voiced concern for them,
I prayed and believed with conviction,
God would save them, only He knew when.

I thanked God for my church, the members,
A special blessing I asked for my pastor,
His family and the elders around him,
May they faithfully follow You, Master.

I remembered the friends that God gave me,
I covered them with His blood,
I confess I neglect them sometimes,
And don't pray for them as I should.

I finally turned my prayers inward,
As God's spotlight shone on me,
I opened my heart to His probing,
For healing where only He can see.

I'm glad that I was obedient,
To what God laid on my heart,
So each day in my devotions,
I will follow my list from the start.

♦

Finally, be strong in the Lord and in His mighty power. Put on the full armor of God, so that you can take your stand against the devil's schemes. For our struggle is not against flesh and blood, but against the rulers, against the authorities, against the powers of this dark world and against the spiritual forces of evil in the heavenly realms.

Therefore put on the full armor of God, so that when the day of evil comes, you may be able to stand your ground, and after you have done everything, to stand. Stand firm then, with the belt of truth buckled around your waist, with the breastplate of righteousness in place, and with your feet fitted with the readiness that comes from the gospel of peace. In addition to all this, take up the shield of faith, with which you can extinguish all the flaming arrows of the evil one. Take the helmet of salvation and the sword of the Spirit, which is the Word of God. And pray in the Spirit on all occasions with all kinds of prayers and requests. With this in mind, be alert and always keep on praying for all the Lord's people.

Ephesians 6: 10-18
Today's New International Version

19.
MY HEAVENLY OUTFIT

It is always such a pleasure,
To buy myself a new dress,
Even though sometimes I wonder,
Maybe I should have paid a bit less.

I love a fresh new hairstyle,
That makes my face look nice,
The nails and the accessories,
They all make up the price.

But today that's not my focus,
Today that's not my plan,
Right now I want to give some thought,
On dressing my inner man.

I want my lips to be praying,
With supplication in the spirit,
I want my eyes to be watchful,
And my life, a heavenly outfit.

I want my heart covered in righteousness,
Not brown that's the color of wood,
I want it wrapped in big bright red,
The color of Christ's blood.

On my head, the helmet of salvation,
As I fill my mind with His Word,
My thoughts are now a consumer,
Of all I've seen and heard.

I'm wearing preparation of the gospel,
Like shoes upon my feet,
I'm wearing a belt of truthfulness,
That fits my waist quite neat.

The shield of faith I will hold up,
To quench those fiery darts,
That the wicked one is always aiming,
He would love to pierce my heart.

For I wrestle against principalities,
Not against blood and not against man,
So when I dress myself in the armor of God,
Then having done all, I can stand.

♦

20.
A Celebration of Praise

I'm putting away distractions,
My eyes are closed and my hands raised,
I'm taking a break for a moment,
To give God a Celebration of Praise.

I'm thanking Him for the wonder,
Of being able to walk, to see,
I want to shout to the whole world,
I am liberated in Christ, I am free.

In a world that's full of turmoil,
I have a peace so deep within,
It's a tribute to my Lord and Master,
For my mind is stayed on Him.

I'm no more easily offended,
For I am grounded in the Word,
You're a conqueror and an overcomer,
Is what my soul has often heard.

I'm growing as my soul prospers,
Moving on from phase to phase,
Each new day is so exciting,
For it's a Celebration of Praise.

◆

About the author
Vicklyn Thomas

For Vicklyn, an ardent fan of reading from a very young age, writing always came naturally. Coupled with the love of poetry, it was only a matter of time before they all came together. Walking with God and desiring to do and be all He wanted for her, has made this a reality.

Vicklyn was born in the Caribbean island of Barbados and now makes Boston, MA, her home. As a wife and mother of two, it is her desire that her work draw others to Christ and strengthen those that already walk with Him.

Some Special Thank Yous

I want to say special thanks to my husband, David, for his unwavering support. He has truly stood by me all the way.

Thank you
To my friend, Sheila Lovell, for
her encouragement,
affirming me as a poet even when I
didn't dare to call myself one.

Thank you to Pastor Lawrence Ward
for his constant urging to take this step,
and to Rev. Jennifer Prescott for
her love and support.

www.ingramcontent.com/pod-product-compliance
Lightning Source LLC
Chambersburg PA
CBHW032136090426
42743CB00007B/619